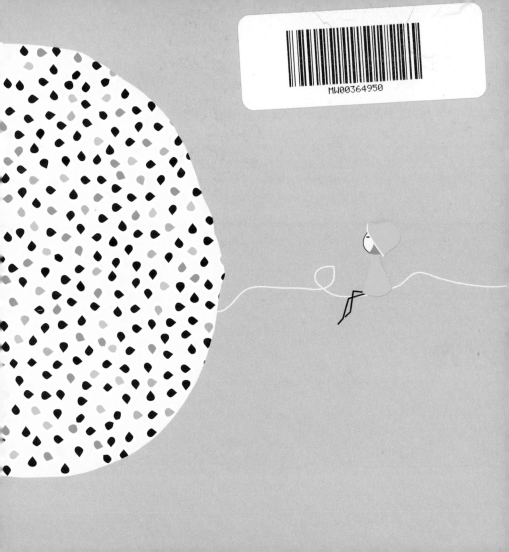

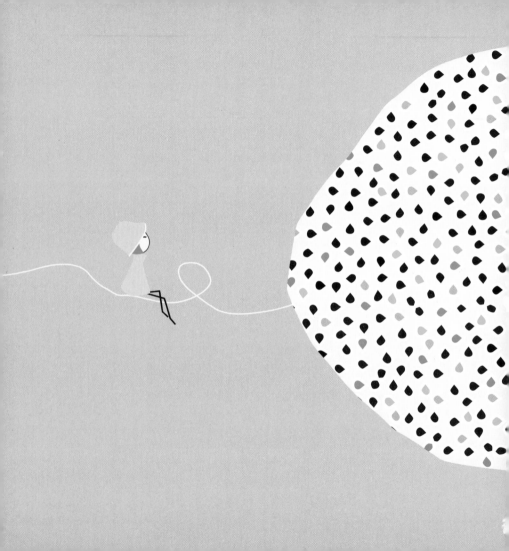

THESE LITTLE GEMS BELONG TO:

....
(*)

....
FROM

(*) THIS IS ME, THE LUCKY ONE!

Published by Sellers Publishing, Inc.
161 John Roberts Road, South Portland, ME 04106
Visit us at www.sellerspublishing.com • E-mail: rsp@rsvp.com

Managing Editor, Mary L. Baldwin
Production Editor, Charlotte Cromwell

ISBN-13: 978-1-4162-4647-3

Printed and bound in China.

10 9 8 7 6 5 4 3 2 1

NINA'S little GEMS

FRIENDSHIP
IS NO
SMALL THING

NINA AND OTHER LITTLE THINGS®
BY ELOISE MORANDI NASH

A FRIEND IS A GIFT YOU GIVE YOURSELF.

. ROBERT LOUIS STEVENSON .

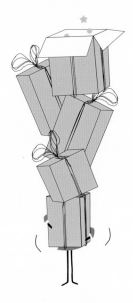

.5.

A FRIEND IS WHAT THE HEART NEEDS ALL THE TIME . . .

. HENRY VAN DYKE .

STRANGERS ARE JUST FRIENDS WAITING TO HAPPEN.

. UNKNOWN .

SURROUND
YOURSELF
ONLY
WITH PEOPLE
WHO ARE GOING
TO LIFT
YOU HIGHER.

. HENRY WADSWORTH LONGFELLOW .

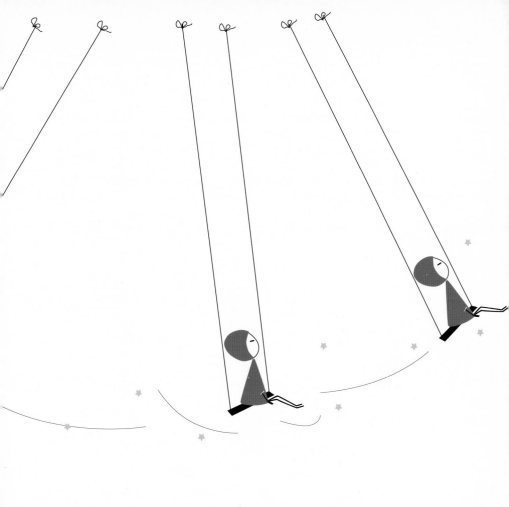

A CIRCLE IS ROUND, IT HAS NO END.

THAT IS HOW LONG I WANT TO BE YOUR FRIEND.

. UNKNOWN .

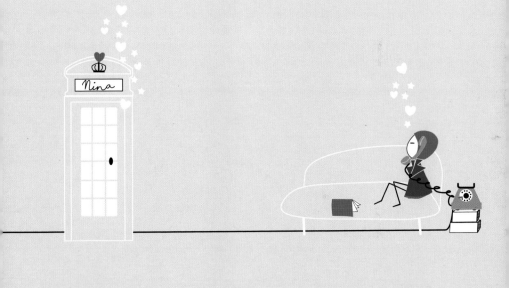

ARE THE

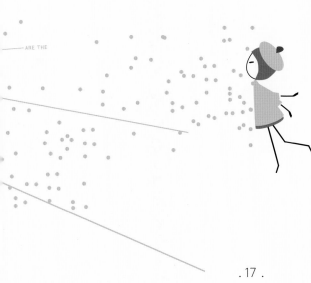

THERE IS
NOTHING BETTER
THAN A FRIEND,
UNLESS IT IS
A FRIEND WITH
CHOCOLATE.

. LINDA GRAYSON .

DON'T WALK BEHIND ME;
I MAY NOT LEAD.
DON'T WALK IN
FRONT OF ME;
I MAY NOT FOLLOW.
JUST WALK BESIDE ME
AND BE MY FRIEND.
JUST BE MY FRIEND.

. ALBERT CAMUS .

THE BEST MIRROR
IS
AN OLD FRIEND.

. GEORGE HERBERT .

A FRIEND IS SOMEONE WHO GIVES YOU
TOTAL FREEDOM TO BE YOURSELF.

. JIM MORRISON .

AH, HOW GOOD IT FEELS! THE HAND OF A FRIEND.

. LATIN PROVERB .

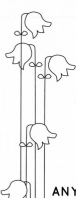

ANYTHING,
EVERYTHING,
LITTLE OR BIG,
BECOMES AN ADVENTURE
WHEN THE RIGHT
PERSON SHARES IT.

. KATHLEEN NORRIS .

ANY DAY SPENT WITH YOU IS MY FAVORITE DAY.

. A. A. MILNE .

LOTS OF PEOPLE WANT TO RIDE WITH YOU IN THE LIMO,

BUT WHAT YOU WANT IS SOMEONE WHO WILL TAKE THE BUS WITH YOU WHEN THE LIMO BREAKS DOWN.

. OPRAH WINFREY .

A STRONG FRIENDSHIP DOESN'T NEED
DAILY CONVERSATION OR BEING TOGETHER.
AS LONG AS THE RELATIONSHIP LIVES IN THE HEART,
TRUE FRIENDS NEVER PART.

. ANONYMOUS .

WE SHOULD ALWAYS HAVE
THREE FRIENDS IN OUR LIVES . . .
ONE WHO WALKS AHEAD
WHO WE LOOK UP TO AND FOLLOW . . .
ONE WHO WALKS BESIDE US,
WHO IS WITH US EVERY STEP OF OUR JOURNEY;
AND THEN, ONE WHO WE REACH BACK FOR
AND BRING ALONG AFTER
WE'VE CLEARED THE WAY.

. MICHELLE OBAMA .

A TRUE FRIEND IS SOMEONE WHO
IS THERE FOR YOU WHEN HE'D RATHER
BE ANYWHERE ELSE.

. LEN WEIN .

WHAT IS A FRIEND?

A SINGLE SOUL DWELLING

IN TWO BODIES.

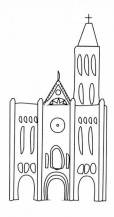

SOME PEOPLE GO TO PRIESTS.

OTHERS TO POETRY.

I TO MY FRIENDS.

. VIRIGINIA WOOLF .

WISHING TO BE FRIENDS IS QUICK WORK,

BUT FRIENDSHIP IS A SLOW RIPENING FRUIT.

. ARISTOTLE .

time care empathy time laughs time advice

FRIENDSHIP IS ...

VERY LONG PHONE CALLS ABOUT NOTHING.

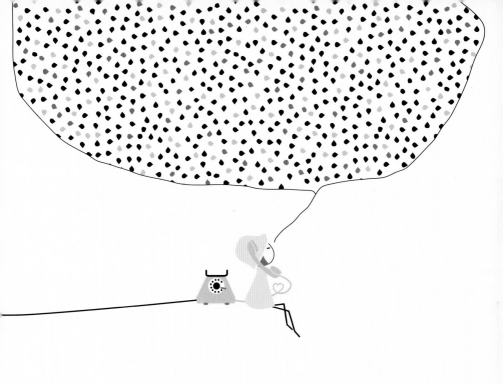

FRIENDSHIP IS BORN AT THAT MOMENT WHEN

ONE PERSON SAYS TO ANOTHER:

"WHAT! YOU TOO? I THOUGHT I WAS THE ONLY ONE!"

. C.S. LEWIS .

A GOOD FRIEND IS LIKE A FOUR-LEAF CLOVER;

HARD TO FIND AND LUCKY TO HAVE.

. IRISH PROVERB .

FRIENDS SHOULD BE LIKE BOOKS, FEW,

BUT HAND-SELECTED.

. C.J. LANGENHOVEN .

SIT BESIDE YOUR FRIEND'S BROKEN HEART,

GRACEFULLY HOLD THEIR TEARS AND TAKE CARE OF THEM.

ONE DAY THEY MIGHT BECOME SPARKLING LAUGHS.

. NINA .

A FRIEND IS ONE THAT KNOWS

YOU AS YOU ARE,

UNDERSTANDS WHERE YOU HAVE BEEN,

ACCEPTS WHAT

YOU HAVE BECOME . . .

. WILLIAM SHAKESPEARE .

AND STILL,

GENTLY

ALLOWS YOU

TO

GROW.

to mum, dad,
my 2 cats,
my friends
and the minds
who came across
my life.

eloise

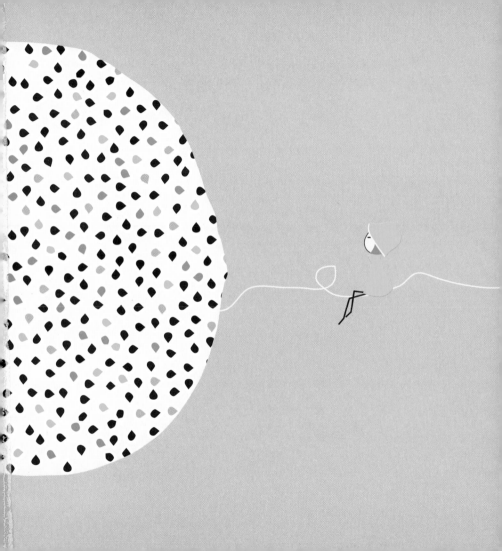